MY FIRST BOOK

AUSTRIA

ALL ABOUT AUSTRIA FOR KIDS

Interior and cover Design: Daniel Day
Editor: Margaret Bam

For My Sons, Daniel, David and Jude

St Michael's Square, Vienna, Austria

Austria

Austria is a **country**.

A country is land that is controlled by a **single government**. Countries are also called **nations, states, or nation-states**.

Countries can be **different sizes**. Some countries are big and others are small.

Hallstatt, Austria

Where Is Austria?

Austria is located in the continent of **Europe**.

A continent is **a massive area of land that is separated from others by water or other natural features**.

Austria is situated in the western part of Europe.

Vienna State Opera, Vienna, Austria

Capital

The capital of Austria is Vienna.

Vienna is located in the **eastern part** of the country.

Vienna is the largest city in Austria.

Holy Trinity column on the main square, Linz, Austria

States

Austria is a country that is made up of nine states.

The states of Austria are as follows:

- **Burgenland - Burgenland.**
- **Kärnten - Carinthia.**
- **Niederösterreich - Lower Austria.**
- **Oberösterreich - Upper Austria.**
- **Salzburg - Salzburg.**
- **Steiermark - Styria.**
- **Tirol - Tyrol.**
- **Vorarlberg - Vorarlberg.**

Woman in Vienna, Austria

Population

Austria has population of around **9 million people** making it the 97th most populated country in the world and the 18th most populated country in Europe.

Size

Austria is **83,871 square kilometres** making it the 21st largest country in Europe by area.

Austria is the 115th largest country in the world.

Languages

The official language of Austria is **German.** The German language is one of the most spoken languages in the world.

Slovene, Croatian and Hungarian are also widely spoken in Austria.

Here are a few Austrian phrases
- **Grüss Gott -** Good Afternoon
- **Pfiat di -** Bye

Schonbrunn Palace in Vienna

Attractions

There are lots of interesting places to see in Austria.

Some beautiful places to visit in Austria are

- Schönbrunn Palace
- The Hofburg
- St. Stephen's Cathedral
- Fortress Hohensalzburg
- Vienna Operahouse
- Mirabell Palace

Austrian parliament

History of Austria

The area now known as Austria emerged at the end of the first millennium from the remnants of the Eastern and Hungarian March.

During pre-Roman times. Austria was settled by numerous Celtic tribes.

On 15th May 1955, The Austrian State Treaty or Austrian Independence Treaty re-established Austria as a sovereign state.

Salzburg Cathedral, Salzburg, Austria

Customs in Austria

Austria has many fascinating customs and traditions.

- Easter is a very popular holiday in Austria. Many Austrians have an Easter egg battle during the family Easter breakfast or brunch.
- Stealing the bride is an old and symbolic Austrian tradition. Friends of the bride and groom crash the wedding to steal the bride. The bride is taken to local bars and is released when the groom pays a ransom which is involves a round of drinks.

Wolfgang Mozart (1756-1791)

Music of Austria

There are many different music genres in Austria such as **Austrian hip hop, Alpine folk music, Austropop, Waltz, Contemporary classical music and Operetta.**

Some notable Austrian musicians include
- **Falco**
- **Parov Stelar**
- **Franz Schubert**
- **Alban Berg**
- **Arnold Schoenberg**
- **Wolfgang Mozart**

Tafelspitz

Food of Austria

Austria is known for having delicious, flavoursome and rich dishes.

The national dish of Austria is **Tafelspitz** which is a boiled beef broth served with horseradish.

Food of Austria

Some popular dishes in Austria include

- **Wienerschnitzel**
- **Brettljause**
- **Gröstl**
- **Klöße Dumplings**
- **Goulash Soup**
- **Kaiserschmarrn**
- **Almdudler**
- **Käsespätzle.**

Gosau mountain village, Upper Austria, Austria

Weather in Austria

Austria is located within a **temperate climatic zone** and has temperatures that are cool year-round in the mountains, and warmer year-round in the cities.

Forest animals in Styria, Austria

Animals of Austria

There are many wonderful animals in Austria.

Here are some animals that live in Austria

- Deer
- Stag
- Rabbit
- Pheasant
- Fox

Hallstatt Village, Austria

Mountains

There are many beautiful mountains in Austria which is one of the reasons why so many people visit this beautiful country every year.

Here are some of Austria's mountains

- Grossglockner
- Kitzsteinhorn
- Wildspitze
- Hoher Dachstein
- Großvenediger
- Weißkugel

Austrian football fan

Sports of Austria

Sports play an integral part in Austrian culture. The most popular sport is **Football.**

Here are some of famous sportspeople from Austria

- **Niki Lauda - Formula 1**
- **Dominic Thiem - Tennis**
- **David Alaba - Football**
- **Toto Wolff - Formula 1**
- **Jochen Rindt - Formula 1**

Famous

Many successful people hail from Austria.

Here are some notable Austrian figures

- **Wolfgang Amadeus Mozart - Composer**
- **Sigmund Freud - Psychiatrist**
- **Arnold Schwarzenegger - Actor**
- **Maria Theresia - Queen regnant**

Main square, Hallstatt, Austria

Something Extra...

As a little something extra, we are going to share some lesser known facts about Austria.

- **The sewing machine was invented by Austrian Josef Madersperger.**
- **The Austrian Alps make up over 60% of the Austria's land area.**
- **Austria is home to Europe's tallest Waterfall.**

Dachstein Glacier, Gosausee, Salzkammergut

Words From the Author

We hope that you enjoyed learning about the wonderful country of Austria.

Austria is a country rich in culture and beauty, with lots of wonderful places to visit and people to meet.

We hope you continue to learn more about this wonderful nation. If you enjoyed this book, consider leaving a review!

With Love

Manufactured by Amazon.ca
Bolton, ON